The Pain I Hide

Ariona Bailey

authorHOUSE®

AuthorHouse™
1663 Liberty Drive
Bloomington, IN 47403
www.authorhouse.com
Phone: 833-262-8899

Published by AuthorHouse 08/05/2021

ISBN: 978-1-6655-3398-0 (sc)
ISBN: 978-1-6655-3397-3 (e)

Library of Congress Control Number: 2021915878

Print information available on the last page.

The Beginning

I put the pen to the paper and just write
Short and long stories about my life

The things I've done, things I've seen
The painful falls, horrible dreams
Tears of pain in a dark lonely room so no one can hear me scream

Thought I knew who I was but truth be
told I am a stranger to myself

As I head off to find me
My reflection in the mirror made me realize,
there she is who was hiding
Behind baggy clothes and a manly walk
With a typical "black girl attitude" and a "hood nigga walk"
Eyes playing tricks on my mind
Those are not my true colors so I guess you can call me color blind

Born for This

Poetry is my natural thing
Like my black and brown curly hair
It's a god given talent
Not for special occasions
It's more of a casual thing
Like when you don't want to dress up but don't know what to wear
But me, I am naked of clothing and have messy hair
Yet my body is covered in words
Words that form poetry
Poetry that speaks of hurt, pain, struggles and lack of love

Hidden Struggles

The pain *I hide*
Deep inside
Makes me feel not so alive
I made it but not sure how I survived

Pain

Heart beating out of my chest
Tears dropping down to the floor
Pacing back and forth, I can't rest
Don't know what to do but I can't take this pain no more

I'm sick of this
I say "I'm depressed and nobody's curious
I'm dying inside and many are oblivious
This is not a game, my heart is serious

Emotional Rollercoaster

I put up a front so that it appears that I
am doing better than my peers
Walking around with a frown on my face
knowing deep down inside there's a frown
With tears of blood because that's how bad my heart aches
My love hidden in the shadow of the ground I walk
Because the ones I thought loved me drilled my heart in the ground
Maybe I was looking for love in all the wrong places
but I've learned love is not to be found
I hate love for not loving me when I was ready to be loved
But if love is ready to love me then come and get me
I love love and if love wants to be loved then love will find me
I am easy to find because I am not hiding

In My head

Fighting my inner me
Not realizing I'm my own worst enemy

Lost in my thoughts
I'm confused mentally
Creating my own insecurities
Trying to understand my true identity

Going Through The Motions

I've been through trials and tribulations
Mind running wild for miles
Got me hyperventilating

Tried to hide my depression
But I wore it on my face
That's the worse facial expression

Got the courage to pick my head up and do it on my own

Down and Out

Looking at my feet
Head down as I walk
Throat dry, I can't talk
As soon as I open my mouth tears fall
Snotty nose, dry face, ears clogged
I just want this pain to stop

Darkness of Love and Life

Tears rolling down my face as I lay in bed
Trying to fall asleep but I can't because of
all the many thoughts in my head
Trying to figure out what's wrong with my life
Decisions Decisions
Don't know what to do to make things right

I'm so confused
Because I've been mentally abused
And I did it to myself which is called self-inflicted wounds

To make it go away I block out everything
around me to focus on what's ahead
And that's a bright future
I put my head on straight
I'm not thinking about what other people tell me
So I'm done living a nightmare
I'm trying to turn my dreams into reality

Not Found

Lost
In A dark place all alone
So many ways out

Lost
In A dark place
On my own
Because I have no place to call home

Lost
In A dark place on my own
In A dark place all alone
Where is my home?

No Self-Confidence

I may appear happy on the outside
Deep down I am broken
I am sad
I am lonely
I'm fired up but my heart is frozen
It's hard for me to trust that's why my emotions were unspoken

No Love Found

No blood left in my heart
Standing here emotionally
Expressing deep emotions
I never thought this would be so hard
Until they ride the wave they'll never understand
"my pain runs deeper than the ocean"

I've been mentally abused
Tried to give people the benefit of the doubt
so a lot of brutalness was excused

I grew older
My heart got colder
No love lose, no love found
Everybody gets the shrug of the shoulder

No handshakes, no hugs
Just head nods and mean mugs

The Misunderstood

They wouldn't understand my pain unless
they've walked a mile in my shoes
But I wouldn't wish that on my worst enemy

I'm able to speak on it now but I still have
to live with the scars and bruise
Heart blown out of proportion, no pain was defused
You love me but you hate me
Which one is it? I'm confused

SO used to being the black sheep
Which made my pain deep

Always been the outcast

I may trip, I may stumble but I'll never fall
"Call me when you need me", They never pick up when I call

I get a voicemail or a dial tone
I don't understand what makes them do me so wrong

Distance I figured would be better for my health
So, I distance myself

You really should keep enemies closer
So, when you do what they said you could never
or become who they said you would never
Your accomplishment will feel 10 times better

The Black Sheep

Eyes bloodshot red
Tears rolling down my face
Heart jumping pout my chest

I need go to guide me in the right direction
So much running through my mind like how I've been made
fun of because of my personality and my skin completion
I've been told only people can judge me is God and
the person I see when I look in the mirror

To love is to be loved and one who doesn't love self can't love others

The Outcast

I stand alone even when there's people right beside me
Because I feel as though I have no place in today's society

I am neither accepted for my mental ability
nor my physical apperance
Which goes to show ignorance is bliss

I am beautiful inside and out
I am sure of this without a doubt

So accept me not for who I try to be
But for who I am
A teenage prodigy

And if you're not
I am proud of me
For being my own person

Not living a script, rehearsing
Just take it one day at a time
Because life is not perfect

Confused

What is love?
Who knows!
It's a good thing I suppose
But if that's so then why does it hurt so much
It's complicated
Headaches and stomach pains
Discombobulation on human brains
A big misunderstanding of people's feelings being understood

Complicated

Life is too complicated
My heartaches bad like I'm constipated
Pacing back and forth contemplating
What's first then what's next
Bending over backwards breaking my neck
Knocking down walls just to fulfill my success

Twisted Mind

I cry from my ears
I see with my heart
I hurt in my eyes
A whole in my soul from years of lies
Got knocked to my knees
So I stand on my hands
Because my life got turned upside down
And I see everything backwards
Right to left
At this point only God can help

Life is Over Rated

I'm stressed out
I'm confused
I feel alone

Nothing I do is ever good enough
Why is it that everything I do is so wrong?
If people are there for me then why do I feel so alone

I guess that's just a figure of speech, nothing littoral
But in my eyes, it's the definition of hypocritical

I never get recognized for my good deeds
People are quick to point out what I didn't do

Yet run to me for their own needs

Then tell me what I should and shouldn't say
I will speak no further
Because at night I lay
My head on my pillow
I pray, ask God for forgiveness and guidance

Friends or Not

I'm my own best friend
But my worst enemy

At war with myself
Don't know what's gotten into me

Me, myself, and I
Because there's no one else

Got trust issues
But mainly with myself

Four Lines

The day is long

The night is young

Life is short

Just like this poem

Tongue Twister

Thinking
I think I'm over thinking
Which means I need to re-think my thoughts
Because what I probably thought
I think it might not have been what I thought
I think my thoughts were thought about too hard

Take A Step Back

Thinking what if I would have done this and did that
My life would be much different from what it is now

Would it be better or worse?
Who knows?
Deepest darkest feelings hidden in these
poems so I don't have to ask who told

I told because my heart was carrying a heavy load
Heavy load, over load, cold and froze

Didn't like that feeling so I had to unload
And let go

Simple Mind

Simple minded people think poetry is just rhyme
It's much more to it if you just take your time
Close your eyes and read as if you were blind
Don't think, just feel
Speak true words of deep emotions
Don't hold back, let go and free your mind

DO I know Myself?

I knew one day I would have to come face to face with myself
Look me in my eye
Take a deep breath before answering
Who am I?

Forgetting Myself

I'm so selfless
And that made me forget who I am
Had a breakdown, got overwhelmed
I felt helpless

So busy taking care of everybody else, I forgot about me
Being looked at like a hero but don't forget
I am human and I have needs

Confession to Myself

It's hard to express feelings to people who are judgmental
I didn't understand my own emotions but I knew it was an issue

Many things going wrong because life was teaching me lessons
Finally admitted I was going through depression

Remember Me

Remember me
I who was a loyal friend to you
When you fell, I held out my hands for you

Remember Me
She who picked you up when you were down?
She who gave you a smile when you had a frown

Remember Me
Well, I remember you

You who turned your back on me
You who stepped on my toes like you had two left feet
You who made me insane
You who brought me pain

Remember Me
I am who you betrayed

I Am Me

No one understands that I am truly different
They don't take time to listen
To the explanation that defines the difference
Between me and you

Apologies to Myself

I'm sorry for the way you've been treated
I'm sorry for the lies and mental beatings
I'm sorry for the pain and heart aches
I'm sorry for the love stories and heart breaks
I'm sorry for the betrayal of trust
I'm sorry for the mixed emotions between love and lust
With that being said
This is an apology to myself
For allowing what others think cause stress on my mental health

Made in the USA
Monee, IL
11 August 2021

75435874R00038